BookLife
freedom
Readers

A PENGUIN'S

LIFE CYCLE

BY MADELINE TYLER

BookLife
freedom
Readers

BookLife
PUBLISHING

©2022
BookLife Publishing Ltd.
King's Lynn
Norfolk PE30 4LS

A catalogue record for
this book is available from
the British Library.

ISBN: 978-1-80155-135-9

Written by:
Madeline Tyler

Edited by:
Kirsty Holmes

Designed by:
Danielle Rippengill

All facts, statistics, web addresses and URLs in this book were verified as valid and accurate at time of
writing. No responsibility for any changes to external websites or references can be accepted by either
the author or publisher.

CONTENTS

PHOTO CREDITS

All images are courtesy of Shutterstock.com, unless otherwise specified. With thanks to Getty Images, Thinkstock Photo and iStockphoto. Frontcover – Kotomiti Okuma. 1 – Kotomiti Okuma. 2 – Roger Clark ARPS. 3 – Martin Leber, vladsilver, Kotomiti Okuma. 4 – Gelpi, Samuel Borges Photography, kurhan. 5 – Leksele. 6 – AndreAnita. 7 – buenaventura. 8 – Steve Allen. 9 – Brandon B. 10 – Photodynamic. 11 – Nick shillan. 12 – Rich Lindie. 13 – Giedriius. 14 – Christian Musat. 15 – Robert Bruce Lilley. 16 – Roger Clark ARPS. 17 – Karel Gallas. 18 – Anton_Ivanov. 19 – robert mcgillivray. 20 – Lyudmyla Kharlamova. 21 – hakule. 22 – Volodymyr Goinyk, ClixTorr, Neil Bradfield, Sergey Uryadnikov. 23 – Creativa Images.

WHAT IS A LIFE CYCLE?

All animals, plants and humans go through different stages of their life as they grow and change. This is called a life cycle.

 Baby **Child** **Adult**

WHAT IS A PENGUIN?

Penguins are a group of birds that cannot fly and spend most of their time in water. They are very good swimmers. Penguins live in South America, Africa, Australia, New Zealand and Antarctica.

EGGS

During breeding season, penguins come onto dry land and form big groups called rookeries. Female penguins stay here to lay their eggs.

Most female penguins lay two eggs during the breeding season. Female emperor penguins and female king penguins only lay one egg. Bigger penguins have bigger eggs and smaller penguins have smaller eggs.

INCUBATION

Penguin eggs have to be kept warm so that they can hatch. This is called incubation. In most species, the male and female penguins take it in turns to incubate the egg by sitting on it.

When emperor penguin eggs are laid, the mother leaves to look for food. The father stays with the egg for two months and does not eat anything. He incubates the egg by keeping it on his feet.

PENGUIN CHICKS

Most penguin chicks hatch after about one month. When the chick hatches, it calls out so that its parents will recognise its voice.

Penguin chicks are born with fluffy feathers, called down. Down is not waterproof and it is very thin, so the parents have to keep the chicks warm.

GROWING CHICKS

As the chicks grow, they shed their down and grow new feathers. The chicks grow very quickly, so the parents have to feed them lots of food.

When the chicks are big enough, the penguin parents both go to look for food together. The chicks are left together in a group.

PENGUINS

Penguins grow all of their adult feathers after about one year. Adult feathers are waterproof, so the young penguins can now go swimming.

When the penguin is fully grown, it will leave its parents. When it is around five years old, it returns to the breeding ground to find a mate. Penguins find a mate by calling out and singing.

TYPES OF PENGUINS

There are 17 different species of penguin. The largest species is the emperor penguin. They are over one metre tall and live in Antarctica.

Emperor penguins

Southern rockhopper penguins

Southern rockhopper penguins have spiky yellow and black feathers on their heads. The penguins are only 50 centimetres tall but can dive 100 metres underwater to catch fish.

PENGUIN FACTS

Penguins cannot fly, but they are very good swimmers. Penguins are the fastest swimmers out of all birds and the gentoo penguin can swim up to 40 kilometres per hour.

Gentoo penguin

Penguins eat fish, squid and krill. They feed their young by regurgitating food. This means the adult penguins swallow the food and wait for it to digest. Then they cough it up and feed it to the young penguin.

WORLD RECORD BREAKERS

The oldest penguin in captivity was Rocky the rockhopper penguin. Rocky lived in an aquarium in Norway and was 29 years and four months old when he died in 2003.

The largest colony of penguins is on Zavodovski Island.
Two million chinstrap penguins come to the island to find
a mate and lay their eggs.

LIFE CYCLE OF A PENGUIN

1
Female penguins lay their eggs on dry land.

2
The adult penguins incubate their eggs for one to two months until they hatch.

4
The fully grown penguin leaves its parents. It returns after five years to find a mate of its own.

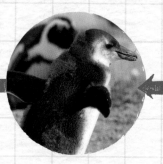

3
The penguin parents keep their chick warm and feed it lots of food. It starts to grow new feathers.

G ET EXPLORING!

Do you want to learn more about penguins? You could visit a zoo or an aquarium to find out about different penguin species.

QUESTIONS

1 How many eggs does a female emperor penguin lay?

   a) 10

   b) 2

   c) 1

2 Who incubates the penguin eggs in most species?

3 How do penguins find a mate?

4 What does regurgitating mean?

5 What is your favourite type of penguin and why?

BookLife
freedom
Readers